Trientrepreneur

A Trient Press Publication for Authors & Entrepreneurs

Issue 3 | june 2021 $10.99

FEATURED
Tom Fargnoli

AUTHOR INTERVIEWS
Interviews with Vito Altavilla and R.J. Waters

TIPS
Must have information for both authors and entrepreneurs

Trientrepreneur
A Trient Press Publication for Authors & Entrepreneurs

$10.99

Copyright © 2021 by Trient Press

All rights reserved. No part of this book may be reproduced or used in any manner without written permission of the copyright owner except for the use of quotations in a book review. For more information, address: info@trientpress.com

FIRST EDITION

www.trientpressmagazine.com

From Trient Press

"I INSERTED A CHIP IN THE BASE OF YOUR SKULL," THE DOCTOR STATED WITH A PROUD SMILE. "I BELIEVE THAT THIS IS HOW WE CAN BRING YOU BACK TO LIFE AFTER YOUR EXECUTION."

June

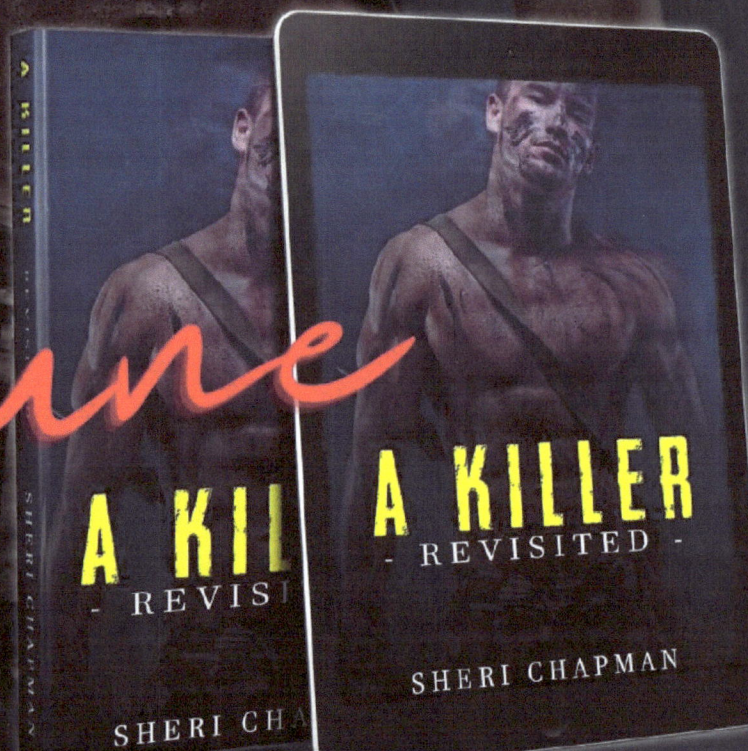

From Sheri Chapman

04 June Author Tips

06 Dark days to helping others

08 Interview with R.J Waters

11 Featured Tom Fargnoli

196 Vito Altavilla

TRIENTREPRENEUR
ISSUE 3

19 The new "norm"

22 The Power of Networking

25 Rock your Audience

27 Advice

35 Resources for New Authors

38 Resources for Entrepreneurs

JUNE AUTHOR TIPS

Writing tips for beginners:

- Make use of time blocks. Research your story in one block; write in another block. You'll make better use of your time when you're focused on one task.
- Don't try to edit when you're writing. Editing requires a different part of your brain than writing. It's impossible to successfully shift between the two, plus it reduces your productivity.
- Turn off the Internet when you're writing. The Internet is a distracting siren.
- Have a daily writing goal. Get specific here. Don't just say "I want to write every day," but create a writing goal, such as 100 or even 1000 words every day.

DARK DAYS TO HELPING OTHERS

Tia Trunk
Cancer

October 21, 2019, I was diagnosed with a blood cancer; Multiple Myeloma. It was unusual for someone of my age, the average age of diagnosis is 69 years. I was a young married woman, with four children and building a business; much too young to leave my family behind.

The Myeloma had eaten holes in my bones and an entire vertebrae. I had to have an extensive 12 hour surgery to replace my vertebrae, a fusion with a 10 inch rod, and 8 screws in my back.

My diagnosis took me to an extremely dark and depressed place. I was crying every morning before my feet even hit the floor. I started having panic attacks, I could only sleep for a couple of uninterrupted moments a night.

→ believe →

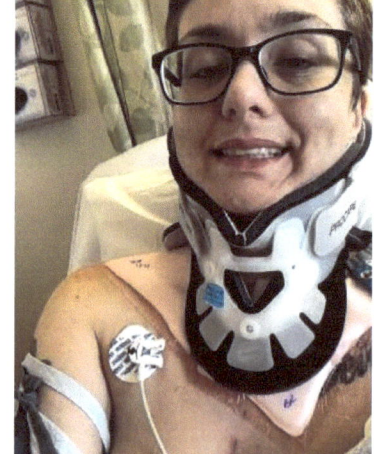

Through the combination of antidepressants and therapy. I overcame the darkness. I promised myself that I would reach out to help others, when I am well. I don't know that I will ever be well. I started Tia Trunk Cancer.

Comfort Gifts to send other survivors and family members, what I like to call "a hug from afar" to let them know that they are not alone. I also have a business (with my partner Kathleen Norris) TK Insurance Solutions, where we focus on assisting families and businesses with their insurance to protect their livelihood. This non profit brings me great pleasure. I am able to be there for people, in a small way, during their darkest time.

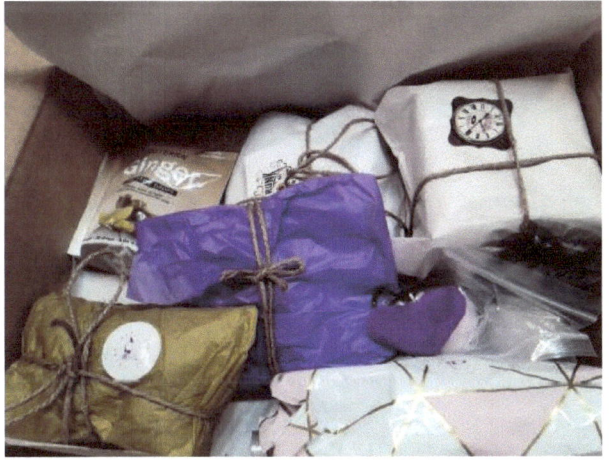

COMFORT GIFTS
during their darkest time

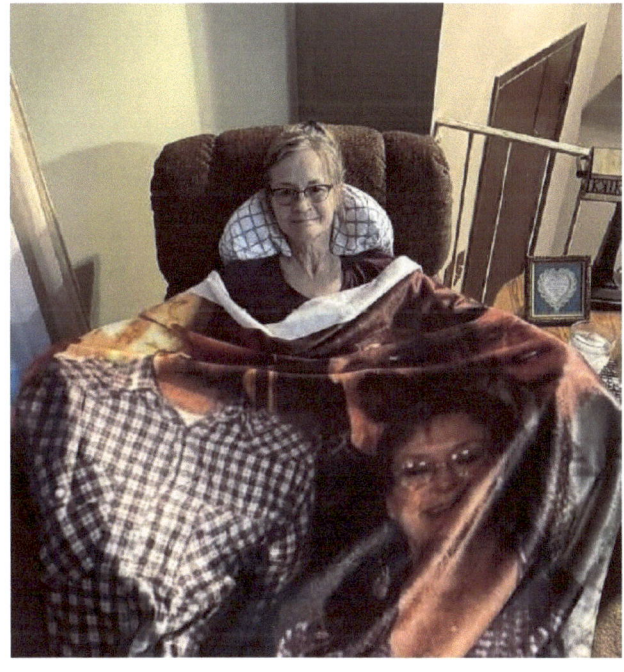

www.facebook.com/TiaTrunk

INTERVIEW WITH R.J WATERS

LYNN: HOW DO YOU PROCESS AND DEAL WITH NEGATIVE BOOK REVIEWS?

R.B: I think you have to consider any criticism with a grain of salt. I don't like every best-selling book or hit movie that comes along and I very often disagree with critics regarding the same. I think you have to keep in mind that these reviews are subjective in that way. Some people are simply not going to like it. As long as I am happy with my work, first and foremost and I enjoyed the process of developing the story and polishing the product, then I have no complaints. If some other people get enjoyment out of it than so much the better.

R.J. WATERS

LYNN: WHAT ADVICE WOULD YOU GIVE TO A WRITER WORKING ON THEIR FIRST BOOK?

R.B: Write every day. Even if only a paragraph, write. Develop your craft and your story. It is all trial and error and no one writes their first draft to perfection, so anticipate you will be editing and changing things as you go, but keep moving the project forward.

LYNN: WHAT PART OF THE BOOK WAS THE MOST FUN TO WRITE?

R.B: I love the action scenes. Having grown up as a fan of comic books, Louis L'Amour novels, and 80's action movies, I am a big fan of fight scenes and like to bring my own creative twists to each and every one. And it is fun to come up with scenarios in which are novel. You can't simply let the book be dominated by gunshots to the head, it gets stale too quickly.

LYNN: WHAT'S YOUR FAVORITE WRITING SNACK OR DRINK?

R.B: COFFEE!!!!

LYNN: IF YOU'RE PLANNING A SEQUEL, CAN YOU SHARE A TINY BIT ABOUT YOUR PLANS FOR IT?

R.B: I am currently writing a sequel to The Unforeseen that will explore more of the relationship between Logan and Paige. Of course, that will be told within more mayhem when Logan is forced to put his skills as one of the premier contract killers to work in an effort to save Paige, his handler, from a group of mercenaries trying to collect a contract on her.

LYNN: IF YOU COULD SPEND A DAY WITH ANOTHER POPULAR AUTHOR, WHOM WOULD YOU CHOOSE?

R.B. : Without a doubt, Micheal Connelly, who I think is one of the best storytellers there is. His characters, plot lines, and his prose are simply some of the best there is today. I would love to pick his brain about style and how he developed characters such as Harry Bosch or the Lincoln Lawyer.

LYNN:WHAT IS THE MOST VALUABLE PIECE OF ADVICE YOU'VE BEEN GIVEN ABOUT WRITING?

R.B. : Don't be afraid of the delete button. Sometimes you are going to have an idea or scenario that simply doesn't fit in the story or picture you are trying to write. Even good ones sometimes need to be omitted to better tell the overall story.

LYNN: WHAT DO YOU THINK IS THE BEST WAY TO IMPROVE WRITING SKILLS?

R.B: Like any skill, practice, practice, and practice. And don't be afraid to hear or accept coaching and criticism.

LYNN: HOW DO YOU COME UP WITH CHARACTER NAMES FOR YOUR STORIES?

R.B.: Most of my character names are based upon people I am acquainted with in some form or fashion. Often times they are named as such because of some character trait those people have that I want to use within a story, though oftentimes the characters are spun beyond recognition by the time the work is done. To me, it is easier to keep track of people and characters I know than to come up with them completely out of thin air.

LYNN: WHOM DO YOU TRUST FOR OBJECTIVE AND CONSTRUCTIVE CRITICISM OF YOUR WORK?

R.B : I have three friends that preview my work. I know all three will be unabashed in offering criticism. As importantly, none of the three are acquainted so I know their feedback is not groupthink. If two, or worse yet, all three, point out the same flaw in something, I know for sure it isn't simply some subjective discrepancy.

To read the full interview, please visit us at https://trientpressmagazine.com/

WOMAN'S BOUTIQUE
CLOTHING & JEWELRY

womansboutiqueclothingandjewelry.com

INTERVIEW

TOM FARGNOLI
Author Interview

LYNN: GOOD DAY TOM, CAN YOU TELL US A LITTLE ABOUT YOURSELF?

I AM A RETIRED ENGINEER, TEACHER, MAGICIAN, AND AN EX-DEACON IN THE CATHOLIC CHURCH. I HAD A GREAT CHILDHOOD GROWING UP IN THE SIXTIES. I LIVED ON MY BIKE AND ENJOYED SO MUCH FREEDOM RIDING ALL OVER TOWN, WALKING TO SCHOOL, TO CHURCH, BUYING CANDY AT A NEARBY CANDY STORE, MAKING MONEY WITH A PAPER ROUTE AND BUYING A HOAGIE FOR 35 CENTS AND A HUGE MILK SHAKE FOR 60 CENTS AT THE NEARBY DELI. I LOVED MY HIGH SCHOOL YEARS TREMENDOUSLY, PLAYING FOOTBALL AND LIFTING WEIGHTS AND DRIVING MY 1954 CHEVY.

AFTER COLLEGE, I MARRIED MY HIGH SCHOOL SWEETHEART AND HAD TWO BEAUTIFUL CHILDREN WHO HAVE CHILDREN OF THEIR OWN NOW. I WAS MARRIED FOR FORTY YEARS, LIVED IN A BEAUTIFUL RANCHER FOR 40 YEARS, AND WORKED AS AN ENGINEER FOR OVER FORTY YEARS. FOUR YEARS AFTER MY WIFE PASSED AWAY, I REMARRIED. I AM NOW LIVING A SMALL TOWN CALLED CLARKSBORO, ALSO IN NEW JERSEY. MY WIFE AND PLAN TO TRAVEL A LOT, ONCE THE WORLD OPENS UP AGAIN. TOGETHER, WE HAVE 17 GRANDCHILDREN.

INTERVIEW

LYNN: CAN YOU TELL US ABOUT YOUR RECENT BOOK?

TOM: My current book, The Deacon – An Unexpected Life, represents my life over the last five years. I was happily married for 40 years and studied to become a Catholic deacon for over 5 years, and enjoyed serving as a deacon for 5 years. It was my dream to be a deacon in my retirement. Life was good – wife, home, children, grandchildren, health, retirement and an amazing ministry. But then, unimaginable tragedy and horror came to my family.

First and foremost, my wife, suddenly and tragically, took her own life. Grieving the loss of a spouse, or any loved one, is devastating but as I quickly learned, grieving is much more complex when it involves losing your love one to suicide. Secondly, when a deacon loses his wife, he cannot pursue another loving relationship that could lead to marriage. I had to commit to a life of celibacy and, essentially, to a life alone. I actually made this commitment before I was ordained, but now, the reality of the rule was like cutting my arm off. I simply could not make a decision and it drove me crazy. – I knew about this rule! This battle went on for almost 2 years – I couldn't decide. It drove me crazy –in fact it landed me in the hospital for open-heart surgery.

My faith was truly being tested, but I managed to hold onto it. But with that decision, came something I never expected. Something worse than loneliness – Rejection – rejection from the church, from some priests, even from some of my brother deacons.

After publishing the book, I was amazed to see how many people were touched by my story and wrote letters to me. People who related to grieving and isolation, people who lost loved ones from suicide, people who struggled with surgery and recovery, people who have faced tough decisions and people who have experienced rejection.

This book is my true story with a touch of fiction to make the story more moving. My goal was to make sure my story moved the reader in the way it moved me. In other words, I wanted the reader to feel my pain, my loneliness, my turmoil, and to relate to it. But I also wanted the reader to experience my faith and my hope and to help them see glimmers of faith and hope despite what they may be going through in their lives.

My message is that is that it is important to focus on those glimmers of light and together with faith, it is possible to journey from the darkness to the light. In my book, I leave the pain and loneliness behind as I journey with God to find my peace and light. In so doing, I find love again and marry again. My wife, Dorothy, also lost her spouse tragically and suddenly. We are both convinced that God, as well as our late spouses brought us together.

LYNN: HAS WRITING THIS BOOK CHANGED YOUR LIFE IN ANY WAY?

Tom: Suicide, Decision and Rejection! Through all of this, my psychologist kept telling me to write things down, so I did! I wrote about my grieving, about suicide, about the decision I had to make, about the rejection, about all of these unexpected events. So what began as a cathartic process, thanks to the Holy Spirit, has turned into my book. Revisiting all of these events as I wrote about them was difficult, but as the book took form, and after reading the first draft, my wife told me that this book is going to help a lot of people. People who relate to grieving and isolation, people who have lost a love one from suicide, people who have had to make life-changing decisions, and people who have faced rejection – they will gain from reading this book. They will gain in seeing that through all of the sadness, that faith can be held on to, providing them a sense of hope and peace. So yes, this book has opened a new chapter in my life – provided me with a tool for continuing to be a deacon, but instead of being in a fancy robe, I will tell stories focused on helping people to see and feel joy in their life, despite unexpected events.

LYNN: WHEN DID YOU FIND OUT YOU WERE PASSIONATE ABOUT WRITING? DO YOU PLAN ON CONTINUING TO WRITE?

Tom: I am currently reading a book called, The Graveyard Book, a novel by and Neil Gaiman. What is interesting about this book is that I am taking an on-line writing class taught by Neil Gaiman and am learning various writing techniques, such as character development and ways to move my readers. I hope to utilize these new skills in my next book. My next book will be a fictional book with a focus on reaching out to those who are yearning to be heard and loved, showing them that, despite their pain, through it, they can grab glimpses of hope, faith, peace and love.

LYNN: HOW HAS IT BEEN FOR YOU DURING THE PANDEMIC?

Tom: As mentioned, my therapist suggested that I write things down. So what began as a cathartic exercise, thanks to being shut-in because of COVID-19, I transformed my unexpected and life-changing events into my book in a rather unique way. In addition, being home has afforded me the opportunity to refocus my life on writing.

LYNN: WHAT MESSAGE WOULD YOU LIKE TO GIVE TO OUR READERS?

Tom: Confucius once said that it is better to save one life than to build a seven story pagoda. You know what's amazing? We put too much time and effort into building pagodas. We live in our heads and not in our hearts. The message in from my story is about a journey from head to heart – we can all make that journey.

We all suffer from time to time – now, with COVID-19, more than ever. We need to know that we are loved – in fact, we are loved more than our ability to understand. We need to reach out to others and build relationships with them and with God.

LYNN: WHAT WOULD YOU SAY IS THE MOST IMPACTFUL PART OF YOUR STORY?

Tom: My book is a story of faith and hope, not only in coping with the loss of a spouse through suicide, but in being forced to choose between remaining a deacon and pursuing another loving relationship. That is all I ever knew – being in a loving and caring relationship for over 45 years. In addition, once I made my decision – a two year battle, I found rejection – rejection from the church, some priests and even some deacons. They treated me as if I left the church or somehow lost my faith.

As the story unfolds, Rick, the reporter who is interviewing me, becomes someone very special. I have strived in this book to help the readers feel that they are a part of my story and will be able to relate to many of my unexpected events. In a way, we all live an unexpected life. My book addresses those events that were unexpected, but also addresses the glimmers of hope that shine through them.

Through writing my story, I have learned that we all need love, compassion and acceptance. I would always tell people at a funeral service that I often conducted, that God lives in our hearts, not in our heads. Writing this book has presented me with a very effective tool in helping people to feel God's presence no matter what they experience in their lives. People can best relate to others who have experienced the kind of things that they have experienced.

LYNN: AND LASTLY, WHERE CAN OUR READERS FIND YOU

Tom: All proceeds of this book go to Suicide Awareness.

My book is available on Amazon and Barns & Noble.

On my website, www.thomasfargnoli.com , your readers will find more about me and more about my current book. In addition, I started a page of me performing some of my favorite magic tricks!

SUICIDE PREVENTION

CRISIS TEXT LINE

Text MT to 741-741
A free, 24/7 text line for people in crisis.

NATIONAL SUICIDE PREVENTION LIFELINE

1-800-273-TALK (8255)
suicidepreventionlifeline.org

INTERVIEW

VITO ALTAVILLA

Author Interview

WHAT INSPIRED THE IDEA FOR YOUR BOOK?

VITO: The idea of actually writing a book came about from Friday morning breakfast meetings with friends (guys) from church. It was always a fun time where we would discuss anything, from; politics to work problems and of course recent humorous events. Of course, once more recent events were brought to the table it would always elicit someone's comment "that reminds me of" and etc.

I always seemed to have more humorous stories than anyone else. After several weeks of breakfast with my friends, someone suggested that I had so many stories that I should write a book. I considered it and decided I would give it a try and consequently wrote this book.

LYNN: CAN YOU TELL US A LITTLE BIT ABOUT YOURSELF?

Vito: I'm a retired industrial research chemist with several national and international patents to my credit in concert with a business partner. My work has given me the opportunity to travel to Asia, Europe, and America lecturing on my technology. However, I realized that humor is everywhere no matter what country. At least in my case and it does not stop as we get older, It only changes. If you pay attention to what you see and experience in life you'll eventually receive more smiles than tears.

LYNN: HOW WOULD YOU DESCRIBE YOUR BOOK'S IDEAL READER?

Vito: I think my book's ideal readers range from forty years old and up. Have at least some sense of humor especially when observing the awkwardness that sometimes people exhibit, physically (general clumsiness) as well as orally (I can't believe he/she said that). An occasional visit to Walmart and you can sometimes witness both of these phenomena in action. I think the older the reader of my book is the more humorous he will find the situation.

LYNN: WHAT PROJECTS ARE YOU PRESENTLY WORKING ON?

Vito: I'm presently working on a sequel to the book. The more I write the more memories come flooding back. I never realized how much I had hidden away.

LYNN: HOW LONG DID IT TAKE TO WRITE THIS BOOK?

Vito: Between rewrites, remembering stories, editing, etc. the book took about six months.

LYNN: WHAT IS THE MOST VALUABLE PIECE OF ADVICE YOU'VE BEEN GIVEN ABOUT WRITING?

Vito: I was never given any writing advice since high school. However, I learned about an environmental element from David Baldacci, Tom Clancy for anticipation, Jack Liondon, for times past and etc.

LYNN: ARE THERE THINGS IN YOUR WRITING SPACE TO HELP YOU STAY FOCUSED?

Vito: Just that computer screen telling me to start. don't dawdle. My mother used to say the word dawdle. Maybe my mother has come back through my computer.
Not serious, just felt a little levity was due.

LYNN: WHAT DO YOU DO FOR FUN/RELAXATION?

Vito: I work out at the gym three times a week and once in a while play some golf and massage my wife's feet and back every night so she goes to sleep with a smile.

www.itbeganinbrooklyn.com

BREAK THE SILENCE. BREAK THE CHAINS.

HELP STOP HUMAN TRAFFICKING

Join the fight at humantraffickinghotline.org

THE NEW "NORM"

BY: KRISTINA WENZL-FIGUEROA

So, there's something that has been weighing heavily on my mind lately and is it just me or has most of the world lost its darn mind? I am not talking about political divides or differences in opinions about healthcare or the issues we face in these trying times; I am talking about the general lack of human decency. Let me explain.

When I grew up—and I realize I am aging myself here—but when I grew up, when I had a problem with someone, I was encouraged to discuss our differences and come to some sort of mutual understanding IN PERSON, not through social media (it didn't exist) or on the phone. What this did was teach me that my way and how I saw things, was not always right and that the other person often had valid points. That in many instances it was possible for both people to be right from a logical standpoint. It taught me to LISTEN. It broadened how I saw the world and make me able to see things from a much larger scope of viewpoints. It expanded my understanding of the world and in turn helped me to grow as a person.

In contrast, now—and I am referring mainly to social media as a generalized platform—when people don't agree, they tend to bully or bash those with opposing views. There appears (at least in my many varied circles) to be a complete lack of empathy or desire to be kind to those who view the world through different lenses. Now, I am not saying everyone I know or even most people that I comingle with are this way; however, there are a few... and my circles are widening. I join many new FB groups, add profiles and new platforms across my varied repertoire of sites I visit daily, and I see it time and time again—this bullying and bashing—with complete lack of embarrassment or shame.

PEOPLE HIDE BEHIND THEIR SCREENS AND YELL FROM THEIR KEYBOARDS.

This lack of any attempt to get to see the other side of things is causing a rift, a divide not just in society but simply between humans. One-on-one.

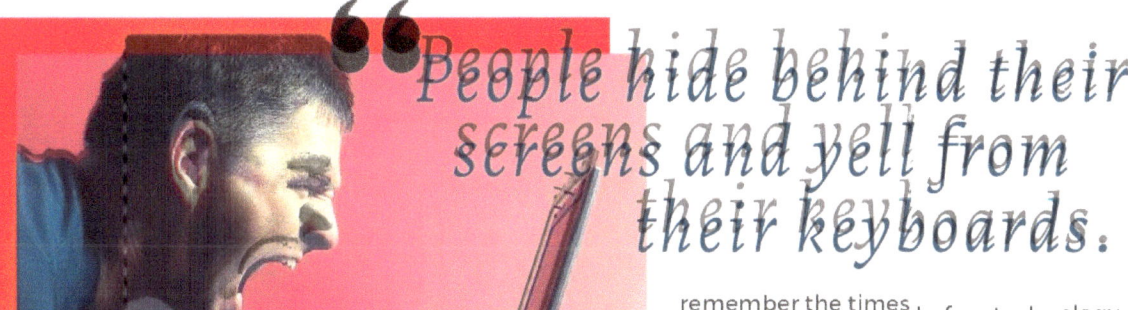

> "People hide behind their screens and yell from their keyboards."

The decency in trying to understand differences seems to be gone. How did it come to this? Sure, everyone feels strongly about this thing or that—but when did it become not okay to listen? When did it become okay to shame others and bully, just because they have different beliefs? NEVER.

It has never become okay, it has just become the new "norm."

So how do we rectify this? Easily, the simplest way is to start with the younger generations, the Millenials, Gen Zs and Generation Alphas. Re-teach empathy, sympathy, and understanding. Somehow the ability to feel for others and see the world from varied perspectives, has gone by the wayside and needs to become a focus.

However, the younger generations are not the only ones to blame. The Baby Boomers and Gen Xers—like myself—need to get back to basics and remember the times before technology. How we were taught to cope, deal, and communicate with others face-to-face. I think sometimes we get so caught up in our lives and with work that decency feels like a commodity that we just don't have time for but being nice to others should never come at so great a cost that we lose sight of the adults we were brought up to be.

I guess I just wish that people did less screaming from their keyboards and did more conscious understanding through their typed responses to others. It takes so little effort and time to be genuinely nice. And, if you find that you really don't want to be or cannot fathom coming from a place of understanding—there's always the age-old adage…

If you can't say something nice, don't say anything at all.

Kristina Wenzl-Figueroa is a full-time business owner, entrepreneur, and homeschooling stay-at-home mom. She loves to write and has several contemporary and adult romances under the pen name, Tina Maurine. You can like and follow her on Facebook, Instagram and Twitter under her pen name or visit her website for more information on her books.

https://tinamaurine.com/

CHANGE ONLY HAPPENS WHEN YOU STEP OUT OF YOUR COMFORT ZONE AND ONTO A NEW PATHWAY.

WWW.JGMACINDOE.COM

POSSIBILITIES ARE ENDLESS, AND THE OPPORTUNITIES ARE BOUNDLESS WHEN YOU ALLOW YOURSELF TO BELIEVE YOU CAN ACHIEVE ANYTHING YOU PUT YOUR MIND TO IT.

I WILL ASSIST YOU IN YOUR JOURNEY OF SECURING DIGITAL BUSINESS OWNERSHIP.

WHAT YOU WILL LEARN

- How to build a foudation for a successful business
- Strategies to automate your business
- Where to get business coaching/ mentoring

ABOUT OUR CULTURE

Imagine the advantage you would gain by plugging into a global community of like-minded digital entrepreneurs.

The Power of Networking

by: Melisa Ruscsak

We often think of networking as pertaining to businesses. For authors and entrepreneurs, the art of networking starts very early on. Networking can actually start in childhood and continue to grow. First experiences are often from teachers that help us become better people. From there, networking connections continue to form from parents, family friends, and others that we meet through our entire schooling years. These first networks are the people that we turn to first when we create an item such as a book or other product.

Not all networking is positive. Most connections formed in these early stages are people we lean on to give honest feedback, both the good and the bad. We relied on them to help us find ways to improve. However, there are those within our First Circle network that will always undermine what we do. Whether misguidance is purposefully done out of spite or jealousy, it is not always given with our best interests at heart. Even if our points of first contacts don't like the product presented or they don't resonate with wanting to support us, in a way, they still do.

Negative feedback is a tool to use to grow. As part of a growing culture, authors must be able to handle criticism and use these points of networking to give us the tools we need to be able to handle negative backlash, critiques, or reviews. So even though it may not feel like it, negativity that surrounds us helps us become better in our craft.

Let's not dwell on the negatives, rather, let's focus on the positives.

Once we've experienced more life, we begin to branch out on our own and start building friends and communities. These can be online through social media. They can be business oriented through places like LinkedIn. They can even be entrepreneurs and business owners from personal communities. We'll call them our second line or Second Circle of Networking.

These are the people that we most closely follow, the ones that give the best advice, and the ones that will help us succeed in our books, our business, or our craft. Your Second Circle will rarely give you negative feedback for the sake of giving you negative feedback. They will, however, give you feedback that will help you grow and give you perspective on how to create a better product. Look at it as fine-tuning your written work or as giving a little push if you're doing something else in the creative world.

Your Second Circle Network will not be the ones that buy your product for the sake of buying it, but once you've fine-tuned your crafts, product, or business, these people will be more inclined to support your business because they believe in it. However, this does not necessarily mean they will invest once your product is ready for the market; they may support it in other ways.

One thing to remember is, investing isn't always about money. It's about investing time and knowledge as well. Once you shine light on what you didn't know, that is when your Second Circle really comes into play. They will be able to provide more knowledge, time, and eventually lead you to the path that provides funding for your company. Even a single author who has a book to sell is a "company". From small to big, a person's company will have its own struggles along the way. It's a comfort to know that your Second Circle will lead to your third and so on. This networking will lead to a community that you need in order to succeed.

This type of networking has helped me personally in my business adventure. My Second and Third Circles helped me create my businesses and attract marketing. My personal experience started from my first tiny Circle. Circle marketing may not work for everyone, but it's a good avenue to try to help get your business off the ground.

ENew, what does that mean? When I started out as an author, my vision was a bit skewed. I wrongly assumed that I only needed to network with people who are readers or other authors. With this philosophy, I will admit, I failed. Yet, I didn't really fail as I didn't have all the knowledge because you don't know what you don't know. So, I started networking with others from investment bankers, entrepreneurs, business owners, etc. going outside my normal network of people to building a network with 2nd and 3rd connections in order to build that essential knowledge.

Once you build a knowledge of what you need to be doing, investment bankers will teach you how to build a business plan. Business plans work great for books as it will tell you where you want your book to be, how many stores do you need to be in, and how many books do you need to sell to reach your goal. Then you look at your investors. That can be anything from retirement investing to building your brand. All of this comes once you start networking with others outside of your normal circle of friends.

So here is a challenge for you. Go to your network and reach out to those second and third connections that you have never reached out to before. Just because you're reaching out to make the connection doesn't mean you're going to offer them anything or buy anything. It means you're going to see what they post and how they post it. See what contents resonate with them. Try to see what works; is it something positive or funny? Is it something that you can take within yourself to build your brand, your book, or your company? Own it and adapt it to suit your needs.

Photo by: Irish Eyes Photography

As I wrote my first book Tighten the Lug Nuts, my vision was simple: I wanted it to be a good read that was helpful and motivating. Additionally, my hope was that readers would see that it was relevant in more than the business world and section of the book shelf. As I read the newspaper each day, watch the news and discuss current events with friends and family, it is clear to me that a core principal that I speak about in the book is more important in today's world than ever before. Regardless of what section of the paper you read, politics, sports, business or entertainment, in the United States or around the world, VALUES MATTER.

Leadership is something we all have concerns about. Leadership is a concept that is not reserved for or only applies to certain people in business, government, or civic organizations. The reality is that no matter our age, gender, occupation, educational level or position in life, each of us touches and influences other's lives. Through this extension we are all leaders to someone at some time. It can be a person under our supervision or care, a spouse we honor and live with, or a child we nurture, a student we teach or a player we coach. It could be as simple as a fellow member of our church or religious affiliation, club, league or association, but it is usually identified by the fact we have made a positive difference through our actions and examples.

Leaders live their values and set the tone from the top. Leadership is not a passive duty - it is an active responsibility. This means providing people with the leadership they need to successfully reach their desired goals in concert with those of the organization.

Values are all about people and managing acceptable behavior. The truth is you're going to have to work at whatever it is you hope to achieve in your life. But it's how you face it that speaks to your character.

Your true character is defined by your honesty of purpose. Your purpose is sacred and authentic. Honesty is what's at the core of your moral character. It's being trustworthy, loyal, fair, sincere and true, even when it is difficult to be. It is not only how you create your values, but also how you add value to the lives of others.

It starts with creating a strong value system, which then must relate to your personal or professional mission and vision. Your personal brand. It must be a guide for all you do. It must align with your personal value system.

In business, it should start with the people you recruit and hire. In your personal life it may be the people you choose to associate with as friends, business partners and acquaintances.

For me this book was a tribute to a wonderful family and it was written in grateful respect for an excellent career that I feel very fortunate and blessed to have lived, learned from, and experienced. It also gave me an opportunity to recognize and say thank you to two very influential people in my life, my dad, Pasquale, and my thoughtful, caring wife, friend, and partner, Debbie Romanella, affectionately known as "the Hon."

As you go through the current events of the day, find those people to thank for their guidance and mentorship and take inventory of all those you have mentored, guided and inspired along the way. Some of you will be very proud, some of you need to get to work. **It all starts with Your Values and Your Legacy.**

Considering the current news of the day, I hope **Tighten the Lug Nuts** can be the book that can help to illustrate **WHY VALUES MATTER.**

One of the best ways we recognize these wonderful influencers in our lives is by recognizing them.

For additional information on these critical topics for success visit our newsletter section at
https://www.3sixtymanagementservices.com/category/newsletters
Pick up a copy of Tighten The Lug Nuts where many of these thoughts and concepts are built out further, **https://tightenthelugnuts.com/.**

ADVICE

I first realized I was clairvoyant at the age of 5. From then on, I had clairvoyance (clear sight) experiences with my mom, on a regular basis. She would look at me, and I would look at her, we would process it as strange, and move on. When I went away to college, I became the resident "go-to girl", for anyone that had a problem, or was feeling bad. It was at this point that I realized that I had a gift. My accuracy could not be ignored and was not just a coincidence or luck, neither of which I believe in. I graduated from the University of Miami with degrees in psychology and human services. Having been a classically trained Ballet and Jazz dancer, I set off to teach my craft. I taught over 25 years, loving every minute. I started a children's dance company for about 13 years. About that time, I fell down a flight of stairs and broke my neck. Yikes! In a year I healed and went on to have both knees replaced, three types of cancer and a mélange of other surgeries. I mention this because the more life threw at me, the better my gift became. I learned through adversity and was given knowledge by the universe, a karmic gift. I am now an Intuitive Psychic, Spiritual Life Coach, Teacher and writer. I possess a keen sense of Intuition, I am a Healer of the Mind, and I work on the undeniable connection between the body and the mind. I have studied Neuroscience and Quantum Physics as they are both relevant to understanding my client's needs.

ADVICE

I bring to you 40 years of experience, and my skill set is strong. I decided to open Intuitive Solutions to share my intuitive gift and help people to find the answers they are looking for. Especially now, as change around us moves swiftly. A sense of calm in one moment can lead to disruption & provoke thought in another. We all wonder.

When I work with a client, I do what is called "hot readings". This means that I start to pick up info when we talk before the reading. This is also true with my Spiritual Life Coaching sessions. Most of my readings take place on the phone and other technological platforms like zoom and skype because energy moves faster than the speed of sound. I also read voices and notice things extremely fast. I provide my clients with answers, solutions, and clarity. Most of us already have the answers, they just need a map and my guidance to get there. I wish to make well being at top of everyone's list.

Dear Holly K

Dear Holly K,
I was thrilled to be able to get both of my Covid vaccines. I can finally breathe a sigh of relief. Almost, my husband is a "male Karen". He feels it is ridiculous, not necessary, unproven and hints at the microchip thing. He is a high school teacher, not virtual. Not only is he completely exposed, our 2 teenage daughters are as well. It only gets worse; he feels they don't need vaccinations either. Any persuasion techniques in your bag of tricks?
Signed,
Mom fearful & at my wit's end

Dear Fearful,
My dear reader; knock it off. You are a grown woman with a mind of your own. Vaccines are now available for age 12, plus. Grab those 2 girls, get them vaccinated. Yes, he is your husband, not your King. Be a great role model for your daughters. Taking matters into your own hands is going to give them a powerful message. The days of bowing to male "rules" are long gone. He will be susceptible (by choice) and you and your daughters safe. Assert yourself. Remember Masks are still necessary in many situations. Here's to your strength and health.
Forever strong,
Holly K

Dear Holly K

Dear Holly K,
Problem, I am conflicted. I need your advice. My Boyfriend has asked me to move in with him. I have been waiting for this patiently for an entire year. I love him very much. One caveat, he is bipolar. That is fine with me...however; he goes off his medication's every few months. All hell breaks loose. He becomes combative, overly sensitive, erratic, the mood swings are akin to a carnival ride. He is great when he is on his meds, he feels good; and decides he doesn't need them. I am not thrilled with the idea of this being a way of life for ME. Please, your best advice...
Signed,
Mentally stumped

Dear Stumped,
You don't sound confused to me at all. The fact that you understand the situation so well; is all the evidence you and I need. Love is tricky, don't let it trick you into a life of futility. Call his psychiatrist and schedule an appointment for you as a couple. Please share with the Doctor everything you have told me. Do not leave anything out. Have your boyfriend share his reasons for the gaps in his medication schedule. Any Shrink worth his weight in gold, will tell you that this is very common behavior for bipolar individuals. You are obviously very smart and mindful; go several times. Also, after these sessions, schedule an appointment for yourself to get all the answers you need (sans boyfriends' presence).

You've got this!
Signed,
Holly K

Dear Holly K

Dear Holly K,
I am a 36-year-old woman. I have my own business. I am successful and financially secure. My question is how long I must wait for a gentleman to share my life with. I know I don't need a man to complete me. Culturally I have been conditioned to really want this, (not to mention the very loud ticking of my biological clock). Online dating is futile and with Covid, well you know what challenges that has created. Holly K, am I destined to live my life as a strong, accomplished single lady?
Signed,
Wanting and waiting

My Sweet Wanting and waiting,
Relax. Nothing happens in the Universe one second before it is supposed to! He is out there, be patient (yes, even more patient). He is on his way. Forget about it, let it go. Release your grip on the steering wheel. The Universe has plans for all of us. Worrying never changes the outcome. In a negative way, it makes us feel a form of control. I promise, as soon as you live in the present (not your imagined future) unexpected things will come to pass. The man that you are looking for will not be the first that you start to date. He is
the second. Chill in the grey. Making things so black and white limits your experiences.
Hang on, keep me posted,
All for love,
Signed,
Holly K

VOLUME OF MIRACLES

THE ANGEL PROJECT

THE JOURNEY

ISSUE 1

A TRIP INTO THE MYSTICAL & METAPHYSCIAL WORLD

DO YOU WANT TO BECOME AN AUTHOR?

Raine Dalrymple
AUTHOR of
"Sight Beyond Sight"

Leap into this COLLECTIVE golden leading edge BOOK with a team of entrepreneurial writers. Bring to the table your INSPIRING STORY of MIRACLES. Share messages that you've had with God, Angels, Visions, Dreams or that of a Loved One's Spirit visiting you. These are the miraculous messages they bring to us. Become an "Emerging Author" in this supportive project.

sightbeyondsight.org

TRIENT PRESS MAGAZINE   JUNE 2021

IT'S SUPERNATURAL

MIRACLES ARE EVERYWHERE

This COLLECTIVE, reciting MIRACLE experiences, entitled, THE JOURNEY is looking for your unique story. Be a LIGHT TO THE WORLD, sharing stories of any experiences you've had of Angel Sightings, Spirits you've seen, Messages you've been given or Mystical Healings you've been a part of or witnessed. Be a part of this Life changing MESSAGE OF HOPE.

BONUSES:

Your name will be entered into a draw for a free spot.

You receive unlimited proofing & editing of your story

Your photo will appear at the top of your page

You receive a free ebook copy

Promotional Advertising globally

The opportunity to gain income

APPLICATION DEADLINE IS JULY 1, 2021
$249.97 CAD
VISIT
SIGHTBEYONDSIGHT.ORG
OR EMAIL AT
SIGHTBEYONDSIGHT222@GMAIL.COM

RESOURCES FOR NEW AUTHORS

WRITERS AND AUTHORS:
Informative Industry Information Sources (Self-Pub and Traditional)

- Poets & Writers
https://www.pw.org/

This website not only provides ready access to databases of literary magazines, small presses, literary agents, MFA programs and writing contests, it also has information about how to get published, and an active community of writers who share information, support, and advice.

- Grammar Girl
https://www.quickanddirtytips.com/grammar-girl

Aptly billed as "your friendly guide to the world of grammar, punctuation, usage and fun developments in the English language," Grammar Girl will set you straight when you're feeling insecure about your use of a semicolon.

- Jane Friedman
https://www.janefriedman.com/best-book-marketing-advice-2017/

When it comes to the topic of publishing in the digital age, there are few people more knowledgeable than former Writer's Digest publisher Jane Friedman. Her blog includes posts on topics ranging from "how to find a literary agent," to "best practices for author Facebook pages," and "the complete guide to query letters."

- Brain Pickings
https://www.brainpickings.org/

If it's inspiration you're after, look no further than this treasure trove of ideas. Curated by the endlessly curious Maria Popova, Brain Pickings is a one-woman labor of love that will provide you endless intellectual and creative stimulation.

AUTHORS HELPING AUTHORS — RESOURCES

Platform, Marketing & Promotion Advice:

Create and verify your Google Business Profile

Get a website

Implement search engine optimization

Create a blog

Share your content

Social Media Post Ideas

- Create a daily, weekly or monthly series
- Run a contest or giveaway
- Host an AMA
- Conduct a social media takeover
- Share, pin, Retweet & regram
- Create bite-sized video clips
- Repurpose your content
- Team up with another brand
- Develop how-to's & tutorials
- Go live
- Give customers the spotlight
- Conduct an interview
- Make a meme

VOLITION
A Uniform & Lace Romance

> " WOW!! What a fantastic book!! This is Noah and Tessa's story and what a story it is!! I HIGHLY recommend this book!!

TINA MAURINE

RESOURCES FOR ENTREPRENEURS

Talking to Customers
- Intercom--tasteful chat and help widgets for your site, plus good automated email triggers
- Drip--email courses and signup widgets for your site
- Mailchimp--newsletters and decent signup widgets
- Buffer--easier way to run your twitter and facebook accounts

Talking to Customers
- Slack--chat and messaging to reduce internal email load, with one room per major project
- Github--repository for your source code plus task lists and collaboration with your developers
- Dropbox--all company files should be here, not on email attachments or personal folders
- Streak--simple CRM plugin for Gmail to manage and share your sales leads
- Trello--digital kanban board for project management
- Basecamp--I use it for project management with external teams who don't know our Trello workflow
- Stormboard--digital sticky notes for remote brainstorming and workshops
- Meldium--team password sharing and management

Payments
- Square (US) or iZettle (elsewhere)--accept credit card payments with your phone, e.g. for market stalls and contractors
- Stripe--best payment processing online
- GoCardless (UK)--accept direct debit payments
- Gumroad--easily sell digital files like PDFs, videos, and links

Analytics
- Google Analytics--free and good enough for all your analytics needs
- Google Keyword Planner--see how many people are searching relevant terms
- Facebook Ads--use the targeting options to compare the approximate size and location of various interests and demographics

Phones
- TextIt--create SMS applications without programming (e.g. for the developing world)
- Twilio--makes phone calls and SMS as easy to program as websites

RESOURCES FOR ENTREPRENEURS

Learning
- Paul Graham's Essays--read the whole archive
- Tropical MBA--250 podcast episodes comprising the best source of knowledge on location independence and manufacturing businesses
- Seth Godin's Startup School--15 audio episodes covering a Seth's take on getting entrepreneurial
- Moz Learn--solid knowledge base on inbound marketing

Investors
- f6s--listing of all accelerator programs (and lots of other info) and a social network for startups and angels
- AngelList--social network and funding platform for startups and angels
- Capitallist--like Angellist, but focused on London and the UK
- The Funded--reviews and testimonials of investors from the founders' perspective; do your investor due diligence here

Crowdfunding
- Crowdcube (UK)--equity crowd funding
- Seedrs (UK)--equity crowd funding
- Kickstarter--crowd-fund via pre-selling your products
- Indiegogo--crowd-fund via donations with a focus on arts and creative projects, including some which aren't allowed on KickStarter

People
- Fiverr--pay $5 (or a bit more) for tasks ranging from logo design to copywriting
- 99designs--crowdsource design tasks (especially logos) for a few hundred dollars
- elance--various freelancers (assume you'll hire several for trial projects before finding good ones)
- Clarity.fm--pay-by-the-minute advice from various startup specialists
- Dribbble--browse designer portfolios, many of whom also freelance

Podcasts Every Entrepreneur Should listen to

The Tim Ferriss Show
https://tim.blog/podcast/

It Will Come Quickly
https://www.youtube.com/c/TheATSJr/featured

StartUp | Gimlet - Gimlet Media
https://gimletmedia.com

Online Marketing Made Easy Podcast with Amy Porterfield
https://www.amyporterfield.com/amy-porterfield-podcast/

Youpreneur
https://youpreneur.com/podcast/

Need help getting booked?

Match Maker FM
https://www.matchmaker.fm/

Command Your Brand
https://commandyourbrand.com/book-a-call-google/

Perfect Podcast Guest
https://perfectpodcastguest.com/

Pod Chaser
https://www.podchaser.com/pro

Podcast Bookers
https://podcastbookers.com/

Pitch Podcasts
https://pitchpodcasts.com/

Radio Guest List
https://www.radioguestlist.com/blog_index.html

Podcast Guest
https://podcastguests.com/

Find Radio Guests
https://www.findradioguests.com/

The Oak Mont Group, LLC
https://www.theoakmontgroupllc.com/how-to-become-a-guest-on-a-podcast/

TRIENT PRESS

Magazine

A Trient Press Publication for Authors & Entrepreneurs

Issue 2 | May 2021 $10.99

FEATURED

A passionate public speaker, army veteran, and businessman. Antonio T Smith, Jr

AUTHOR INTERVIEWS

Interviews with R.B Carr and Claerie Kavanaugh

TIPS

Must have information for both authors and entrepreneurs

GUEST ARTICLES

Have something to share with Authors and Entrepreneurs submit a story to: info@trientmagaize.com

INTERVIEWS

For radio interviews there is a fee: https://calendly.com/mlruscsak-ceo/30min

For free printed interviews Contact Info@trientpress.com

HORROR

ERNEST Roberson Sr.

SUSPENSE

Trientrepreneur

A Trient Press Magazine for Authors & Entrepreneurs

Introducing The Trient Foreign Language Editions

@trientpress
@trientpress

TRIENTPRESSMAGAZINE.COM
TRIENTPRESSMAGAZINE.COM

www.ingramcontent.com/pod-product-compliance
Lightning Source LLC
Chambersburg PA
CBHW051928210526

45473CB00006B/2173